This is my story...

Name: .... *

Date: ....

Every Scripture

Tells a Story

Devotional Thought Journal *for* Women

BARBOUR BOOKS
An Imprint of Barbour Publishing, Inc.

Published by Barbour Books, an imprint of Barbour Publishing, Inc., 1810 Barbour Drive, Uhrichsville, Ohio 44683, www.barbourbooks.com

Our mission is to inspire the world with the life-changing message of the Bible.

Member of the
Evangelical Christian
Publishers Association

Printed in China.

Introduction

Did you know that God's Word is woven into your very own amazing story? . . . The story of YOU!

Think about it. . .

God created you.

He has specific plans for you.

He gifted you with talents to use for His kingdom.

He sent His One and only Son to die for you.

And, at this very moment, He is preparing a home in heaven for you.

This devotional thought journal features prompts related to specific scripture selections that will help you begin to write out your very own story and see how the Word of God speaks truth and love into your life today (and, in fact, from the very moment God first thought of you!).

While each of the journal sections may not apply to your life *right now*, they certainly may play a part in your future—because God is still busy writing your life adventure. So flip to the sections that interest you the most and begin to record your story—with your hand in God's, He'll be beside you each step of your journey.

Be blessed!

Contents

Section 1:

Here's how my story began. . .

Every great story has an epic beginning.
And my story is no different. . .

You made all the delicate, inner parts of my
body and knit me together in my mother's womb.
Thank you for making me so wonderfully complex!
Your workmanship is marvelous—how well I know it.
You watched me as I was being formed in utter seclusion,
as I was woven together in the dark of the womb.
You saw me before I was born.
Every day of my life was recorded in your book.
Every moment was laid out
before a single day had passed.
Psalm 139:13–16 NLT

God had a plan for me from
the very start of my life.

I was born on ....

At this time of day ....

In .... (place of birth).

To .... (mother)

and .... (father).

My full given name is ....

Do you know any details about the day you were born?
Write your birth story here.

....

....

....

....

....

....

....

....

....

....

....

....

....

....

....

....

....

....

....

....

Do you have photos and videos of the day you were born?
How does it make you feel when you look at or watch them?

....
....
....
....
....
....
....
....
....
....
....
....
....
....
....
....
....

So give your father and mother joy!
May she who gave you birth be happy.
PROVERBS 23:25 NLT

11

If you were adopted, share your adoption story here.

_____
_____
_____
_____
_____
_____
_____
_____
_____
_____
_____
_____
_____
_____
_____
_____
_____
_____
_____

"I will not leave you as orphans; I will come to you."
JOHN 14:18 ESV

Section 2:

My name is part of my story.

A good name
is to be chosen
rather than great riches,
and favor is better
than silver or gold.

PROVERBS 22:1 ESV

My parents chose my name because

My name means

,

and that inspires me because

What do you like about your name? If you dislike it,
what would you change it to if you could?

Do you have any nicknames? List each one,
who gave it to you, and how it makes you feel.

Section 3:

I am wonderfully made.

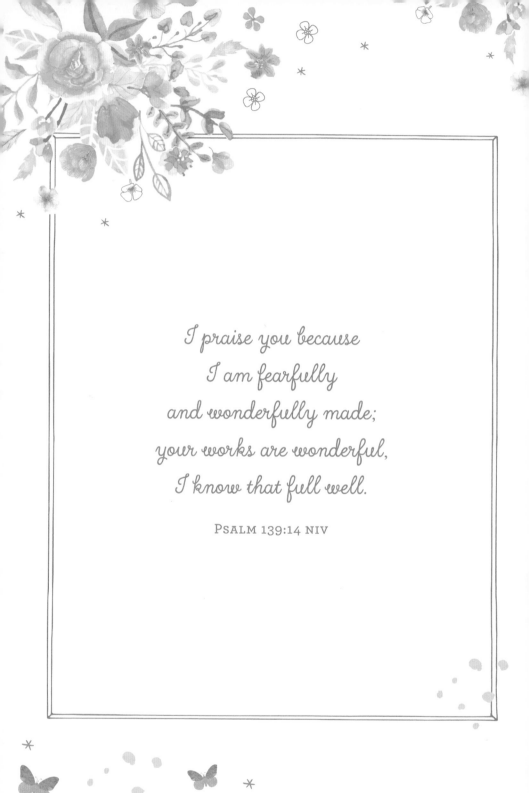

I praise you because
I am fearfully
and wonderfully made;
your works are wonderful,
I know that full well.

PSALM 139:14 NIV

God created me with .... hair,

.... eyes, and ....

....

....

When I look in the mirror I feel ....

....

....

....

....

....

....

....

....

....

....

....

....

....

....

....

....

....

So God created man in his own image,
in the image of God he created him;
male and female he created them.
GENESIS 1:27 ESV

From my mom, I have inherited these physical features ....

....

and these personality traits ....

....

What do you most appreciate about these features and traits?

From my dad, I have inherited these physical features ....

....

....

and these personality traits ....

....

....

What do you most appreciate about these features and traits?

....

....

....

....

....

....

....

....

....

....

....

....

....

....

....

....

....

....

What personality traits of yours stand out
and are different from those of your parents?

....

....

....

....

....

....

....

....

....

....

....

....

....

....

....

....

....

....

....

*"The LORD doesn't see things the way you see them.
People judge by outward appearance,
but the LORD looks at the heart."*

1 SAMUEL 16:7 NLT

People often say I look just like ...., and

that makes me feel ....

....

....

....

....

....

....

....

....

....

People often say I act just like ...., and

that makes me feel ....

....

....

....

....

....

....

....

....

....

....

....

....

Do you believe that you are fearfully and wonderfully made?
Why or why not?

....
....
....
....
....
....
....
....
....

In what ways can you remind yourself of this
fact and celebrate who God made you to be?

....
....
....
....
....
....
....
....
....

Write a response to the following scripture:

And yet, O LORD, you are our Father. We are the clay,
and you are the potter. We all are formed by your hand.
ISAIAH 64:8 NLT

What does it mean to be beautiful?

....

....

....

....

....

....

....

....

....

....

....

....

....

....

....

....

*Don't be concerned about the outward beauty of fancy
hairstyles, expensive jewelry, or beautiful clothes.
You should clothe yourselves instead with the beauty
that comes from within, the unfading beauty of a
gentle and quiet spirit, which is so precious to God.*

1 PETER 3:3–4 NLT

28

Do you care about outward beauty or inward beauty?
Which is more important to you and why?

....

....

....

....

....

....

....

....

What are your thoughts about beauty in our culture today?

....

....

....

....

....

....

....

....

....

....

....

....

How do you strive to keep the right perspective
about what true beauty is and is not?

Section 4:

My faith is the best part of my story.

If you declare with your mouth, "Jesus is Lord," and believe in your heart that God raised him from the dead, you will be saved. For it is with your heart that you believe and are justified, and it is with your mouth that you profess your faith and are saved.

ROMANS 10:9–10 NIV

I became a Christian at .... years old.

Describe your experience of accepting Jesus as Lord of your life.

In what ways has your faith grown since you became a Christian?

....
....
....
....
....
....
....
....
....
....
....
....
....
....
....
....
....
....
....
....
....

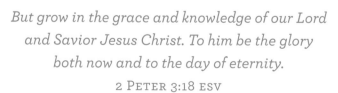

But grow in the grace and knowledge of our Lord
and Savior Jesus Christ. To him be the glory
both now and to the day of eternity.

2 PETER 3:18 ESV

Can others tell that you are a Christian? In what ways?
How do you live out your faith and share it with others?

Worship Christ as Lord of your life. And if someone asks about your hope as a believer, always be ready to explain it.
1 PETER 3:15 NLT

How is the fruit of the Spirit evident in your life?

....

....

....

....

....

....

....

....

....

....

....

....

....

....

....

....

....

....

....

....

But the fruit of the Spirit is love, joy, peace, patience,
kindness, goodness, faithfulness, gentleness,
self-control; against such things there is no law.
GALATIANS 5:22–23 ESV

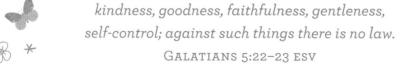

Have any events or circumstances in your
life caused you to question your faith?

The name of my church is ....

I love this church because ....

....

....

....

....

....

....

....

....

....

....

....

....

....

....

....

....

*Let us hold unswervingly to the hope we profess, for he who
promised is faithful. And let us consider how we may spur
one another on toward love and good deeds, not giving
up meeting together, as some are in the habit of doing,
but encouraging one another—and all the more
as you see the Day approaching.*

HEBREWS 10:23–25 NIV

The ways I give and serve and worship in this church are ....

....

....

....

....

....

....

....

....

....

....

....

....

....

....

....

....

....

....

Serve the LORD with gladness!
Come into his presence with singing!
PSALM 100:2 ESV

What are your spiritual gifts? How are they evident in your life, and how do you use them to bring glory to God and serve others?

....
....
....
....
....
....
....
....
....
....
....
....
....
....
....
....

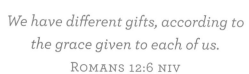

*We have different gifts, according to
the grace given to each of us.*
ROMANS 12:6 NIV

Have you traveled anywhere on mission trips?
If so, how did they impact your faith and your life?

....
....
....
....
....
....
....
....
....
....
....
....
....
....
....
....
....
....

*The Scriptures say, "How beautiful are the
feet of messengers who bring good news!"*
ROMANS 10:15 NLT

I feel closest to God when

Jesus often withdrew to lonely places and prayed.
LUKE 5:16 NIV

I have experienced these miracles in my life:

....
....
....
....
....
....
....
....
....
....
....
....
....
....
....
....
....

Your ways, God, are holy.
What god is as great as our God?
You are the God who performs miracles;
you display your power among the peoples.
PSALM 77:13–14 NIV

My favorite scripture is .... ,

because ....

....

....

....

....

....

....

....

My favorite worship song is .... ,

because ....

....

....

....

....

....

....

....

....

My favorite ways and places to worship God are

Describe the ways you stay committed
to your faith in Jesus Christ.

*Cling to your faith in Christ,
and keep your conscience clear.*
1 TIMOTHY 1:19 NLT

Section 5:

My family is part of my story.

Let love be genuine. Abhor what
is evil; hold fast to what is good.
Love one another with brotherly
affection. Outdo one another
in showing honor.

ROMANS 12:9–10 ESV

What does the word *family* mean to you?

....

....

....

....

....

....

....

....

....

How does thinking about your family make you feel?

....

....

....

....

....

....

....

....

....

....

....

....

These words best describe my mom: ....

....

....

....

....

....

....

....

My earliest memory of my mom is ....

....

....

....

....

....

....

....

....

....

....

....

I feel most loved by my mom when she ....

....

....

....

....

....

....

....

....

....

....

....

....

....

....

....

....

....

Her children rise up and call her blessed.
PROVERBS 31:28 ESV

I have conflict with my mom when

We work it out by

My favorite things to do with my mom are ....

....

....

....

....

....

....

....

My mom inspires me because ....

....

....

....

....

....

....

....

....

....

....

The best advice my mom ever gave me is ....

....

....

....

....

....

....

....

....

....

....

....

....

....

....

....

....

....

....

Don't neglect your mother's instruction.
PROVERBS 6:20 NLT

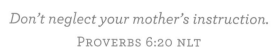

Describe how your relationship with your mom
has developed and changed over the years.

These words best describe my dad:

··

··

··

··

··

··

··

··

What I love most about my dad is

··

··

··

··

··

··

··

··

I feel most loved by my dad when he

....

....

....

....

....

....

....

....

....

....

....

....

....

....

....

....

....

As a father shows compassion to his children,
so the LORD *shows compassion to those who fear him.*
PSALM 103:13 ESV

I have conflict with my dad when

We work it out by

My favorite things to do with my dad are

My dad inspires me because

The best advice my dad ever gave me is ....

....

....

....

....

....

....

....

....

....

....

....

....

....

....

....

....

....

Listen to your father who gave you life.
PROVERBS 23:22 ESV

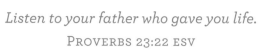

Describe how your relationship has
changed with your dad over the years.

I have .... (number of) siblings.

Are your siblings older, younger, or both? ....

....

....

....

....

....

Describe your relationships with your siblings and how
birth order has affected your relationships.

....

....

....

....

....

....

....

....

....

....

....

....

....

My favorite ways to spend time with my siblings are

What causes the most conflict with your siblings and
how do you work it out?

My siblings inspire and/or help me in these ways:

_____

_____

_____

_____

_____

_____

_____

_____

_____

_____

_____

_____

_____

_____

_____

_____

_____

_____

*Most important of all, continue to show deep love
for each other, for love covers a multitude of sins.*
1 PETER 4:8 NLT

If you don't have siblings, do you wish you did?
Or are you happy being an only child?

My grandparents' names are

....

....

....

....

....

....

Describe your relationships with your grandparents.

....

....

....

....

....

....

....

....

....

....

....

....

....

....

What wisdom have you gained from your relationships with your grandparents?

....
....
....
....
....
....
....
....
....
....
....
....
....
....
....
....
....
....
....

Gray hair is a crown of glory;
it is gained in a righteous life.
PROVERBS 16:31 ESV

Share a favorite activity you've enjoyed with grandparents.

Share a favorite memory you have with grandparents.

....

....

....

....

....

....

....

....

....

....

....

....

....

....

....

....

....

....

*Grandchildren are the crown of the aged,
and the glory of children is their fathers.*
PROVERBS 17:6 ESV

My closest aunts and uncles are ....
....
....
....
....
....
....

Describe your relationships with your aunts and uncles.

....
....
....
....
....
....
....
....
....
....
....
....
....
....
....
....

My favorite activities/memories with my aunts and uncles are

My closest cousins are

....

....

....

....

....

....

Describe your relationships with your closest cousins.

....

....

....

....

....

....

....

....

....

....

....

....

....

My favorite activities/memories with my cousins are

Have you ever lost a family member?
How did you grieve their loss?
How do you honor their lives?

....
....
....
....
....
....
....
....
....
....
....
....
....
....
....
....
....
....
....
....

*"Blessed are those who mourn,
for they shall be comforted."*
MATTHEW 5:4 ESV

Section 6:

My education is part of my story.

Fear of the LORD is the foundation
of true knowledge, but fools
despise wisdom and discipline.

PROVERBS 1:7 NLT

I went to .... Elementary School during these

years: ....

I went to .... Middle School during these

years: ....

I went to .... High School during these years:

....

I went to .... College/University during these

years: ....

My school mascots were ....

....

....

....

....

....

....

....

....

....

....

....

....

....

For the Lord gives wisdom; from his mouth come
knowledge and understanding.
PROVERBS 2:6 ESV

My favorite subjects in elementary school were

because

My favorite teachers in elementary school were

because

Describe the subjects and teachers you struggled
with the most in elementary school and why.

....
....
....
....
....
....
....
....
....
....
....
....
....
....
....
....
....
....
....
....
....
....

Share a favorite memory from elementary school.

My favorite subjects in middle school were ....

....

....

....

....

because ....

....

....

....

....

My favorite teachers in middle school were ....

....

....

because ....

....

....

....

....

....

....

Describe the subjects and teachers you struggled
with the most in middle school and why.

Share a favorite memory from middle school.

My favorite subjects in high school were ....

....

....

....

....

because ....

....

....

....

....

My favorite teachers in high school were ....

....

....

....

....

because ....

....

....

....

....

Describe the subjects and teachers you struggled
with the most in high school and why.

Share a favorite memory from high school.

Did you attend college and/or higher education?

....
....
....
....

Where?

....
....
....
....

What is your degree and in what field?

....
....
....
....
....

Describe your college experience and your course of study...
or describe why you chose not to attend college.

....
....
....
....
....
....
....

Is it important to you to continue to strive to
learn and grow as an adult? Why or why not?

....

....

....

....

....

....

....

....

....

....

....

....

....

....

....

....

*Let the wise hear and increase in learning,
and the one who understands obtain guidance.*
PROVERBS 1:5 ESV

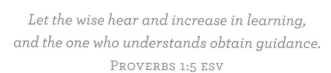

Section 7:

My jobs and career are part of my story.

Work willingly at whatever you do, as though you were working for the Lord rather than for people. Remember that the Lord will give you an inheritance as your reward, and that the Master you are serving is Christ.

COLOSSIANS 3:23–24 NLT

My first paid job was ....

....

....

....

....

....

What did you enjoy about it?

....

....

....

....

....

....

....

....

What did you least like about it?

....

....

....

....

....

....

Share your favorite experiences at various jobs you've held.

Did your college education prepare you well for your career?
Why or why not?

....
....
....
....
....
....
....
....
....
....
....
....
....
....
....
....
....
....
....
....
....
....
....

I find my career very rewarding because

....

....

....

....

....

....

....

....

....

If I could change something about my career, it would be

....

....

....

....

....

....

....

....

....

....

Section 8:

My husband is part of my story.

For a husband is the head of his wife as Christ is the head of the church. . . . So you wives should submit to your husbands in everything. For husbands, this means love your wives, just as Christ loved the church. He gave up his life for her to make her holy and clean, washed by the cleansing of God's word. . . . In the same way, husbands ought to love their wives as they love their own bodies. For a man who loves his wife actually shows love for himself.

EPHESIANS 5:23–26, 28 NLT

My husband's name is ....

We met on .... (date) at ....

Share the details of when and how you met.

....

....

....

....

....

....

....

....

....

....

....

....

....

....

....

....

....

....

....

My husband and I started dating on ....

Choose one word to describe your first date.

....

Share the little details of your first date.

....
....
....
....
....
....
....
....
....
....
....
....
....
....
....
....
....
....
....
....
....
....

What attracted you to your husband?

....
....
....
....
....
....
....
....

What made you say yes to another date?

....
....
....
....
....
....
....
....
....
....
....
....
....
....
....

What were some of the conflicts you had to work through as you were dating?

....
....
....
....
....
....
....
....
....
....
....
....
....
....
....
....
....
....
....
....
....
....
....

Share a favorite memory from your dating days.

My husband and I got engaged on .... at
.... (place).

Share the little details of your engagement story.

....

....

....

....

....

....

....

....

....

....

....

....

....

....

....

....

....

....

....

....

....

....

Did you pick your engagement ring out together or did
he surprise you? Describe your engagement ring.

What words best describe your husband?

....

....

....

....

....

....

....

....

What qualities in your husband made you feel
confident in saying yes when he proposed?

....

....

....

....

....

....

....

....

....

....

Share a favorite memory from your engagement.

....

....

....

....

....

....

....

....

....

....

....

....

....

....

....

....

....

....

....

*For as a young man marries a young woman, so shall
your sons marry you, and as the bridegroom rejoices
over the bride, so shall your God rejoice over you.*
ISAIAH 62:5 ESV

105

Did you attend premarriage counseling?
What resources did you find most helpful?

....
....
....
....
....
....
....
....
....

What did you learn? Did you feel equipped
well for the reality of marriage?

....
....
....
....
....
....
....
....
....

What were some conflicts you had to
work through during your engagement?

Did you have a bridal shower?

....
....
....
....
....

Who hosted it for you?

....
....
....
....
....

What were the decorations and theme?

....
....
....
....
....

What were some of your favorite gifts?

....
....
....
....
....

What did you love most about wedding planning?
What did you find most stressful?

....
....
....
....
....
....
....
....
....
....
....
....
....
....
....
....
....
....
....
....
....
....
....
....

My husband and I married on .... at ....
(place) by .... (name of officiant).
Describe the details of your wedding décor and location.

List the names of those in your wedding party:

....
....
....
....
....
....
....
....
....

Why did you choose these people to share in your special day?

....
....
....
....
....
....
....
....
....
....
....
....

Describe your wedding dress and your wedding party's attire.

....

....

....

....

....

....

....

....

....

How did you know "the dress" was the right one?

....

....

....

....

....

....

....

....

....

Describe your wedding ceremony.
In what ways did you make it unique?

....
....
....
....
....
....
....
....
....
....
....
....
....
....
....
....
....
....
....
....
....
....
....
....

What was the most stressful part about your wedding day?

What was your favorite part of your wedding day?

....
....
....
....
....
....
....
....
....
....
....
....
....
....
....
....
....
....
....

*He who finds a wife finds a good thing
and obtains favor from the Lord.*
PROVERBS 18:22 ESV

For our honeymoon, we traveled to ....

....

....

....

....

....

....

....

....

Describe favorite memories from your trip.

....

....

....

....

....

....

....

....

....

We came home from our honeymoon to ....

(address)

Describe your first home together.

....
....
....
....
....
....
....
....
....
....
....
....
....
....
....
....
....
....
....
....
....
....

What life event(s) affected your marriage in the worst way?

What life event(s) affected your marriage in the best way?

What has surprised you most about marriage?

Let marriage be held in honor among all.
HEBREWS 13:4 ESV

What causes the most conflict in your marriage?
How do you work it out?

....

....

....

....

....

....

....

....

....

....

....

....

....

....

....

....

....

....

....

....

*Love bears all things, believes all things,
hopes all things, endures all things.*
1 CORINTHIANS 13:7 ESV

What causes the most joy in your marriage?

....

....

....

....

....

....

What makes you feel the most loved in your marriage?

....

....

....

....

....

....

How do you continue to cultivate a good
relationship with your husband?

....

....

....

....

....

....

Section 9:

My children are part of my story.

Children are a gift from the LORD;
they are a reward from him.

PSALM 127:3 NLT

But Jesus said, "Let the children
come to me. Don't stop them!
For the Kingdom of Heaven belongs
to those who are like these children."

MATTHEW 19:14 NLT

My children's names and birthdates:

Describe the birth stories of each of your children.

Describe the personalities of and your
relationships with each of your children.

Describe the relationships of each of your children with each other.

What is your favorite part of being a mom?

What is the most difficult/challenging part of being a mom?

....

....

....

....

....

....

....

....

....

....

....

....

....

....

....

....

....

....

....

....

Direct your children onto the right path,
and when they are older, they will not leave it.
PROVERBS 22:6 NLT

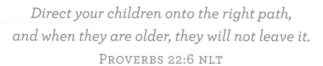

What are your favorite things to do with your children?

What makes you feel most loved by your children?

How would you describe your parenting style?
How is it similar to or different from the way you were raised?

How does your walk with God and your love for His
Word determine the way you parent your children?

....

....

....

....

....

....

....

....

....

....

....

....

....

....

....

....

....

....

Discipline your son, and he will give you rest;
he will give delight to your heart.
PROVERBS 29:17 ESV

What causes the most conflict with your
children, and how do you work it out?

What are your dreams for your children?

What do you pray most for your children?

....
....
....
....
....
....
....
....
....
....
....
....
....
....
....
....
....
....
....

I have no greater joy than to hear that
my children are walking in the truth.

3 JOHN 1:4 ESV

Section 10:

My friends are part of my story.

Two people are better off than one, for they can help each other succeed. If one person falls, the other can reach out and help. But someone who falls alone is in real trouble. Likewise, two people lying close together can keep each other warm. But how can one be warm alone? A person standing alone can be attacked and defeated, but two can stand back-to-back and conquer. Three are even better, for a triple-braided cord is not easily broken.

ECCLESIASTES 4:9–12 NLT

One of my closest friends is ....

Describe your friendship. What connected you in
the beginning and what keeps you connected today?

....

....

....

....

....

....

....

....

....

....

....

....

....

....

....

....

....

....

....

Another of my closest friends is ....

Describe your friendship. What connected you in
the beginning and what keeps you connected today?

Yet another of my closest friends is ....

Describe your friendship. What connected you in
the beginning and what keeps you connected today?

Share your favorite memories from childhood friendships.

....

....

....

....

....

....

....

....

....

....

....

....

....

....

....

....

*Therefore encourage one another and build
one another up, just as you are doing.*
1 THESSALONIANS 5:11 ESV

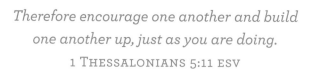

Share an experience of when a friendship ended.
What did you learn from that experience?

Have you experienced the death of a friend? How did you grieve
the loss? How do you honor the life of that friend now?

What qualities make a good friend? Do you
feel like you are a good friend to others?

....
....
....
....
....
....
....
....
....
....
....
....
....
....
....
....
....
....
....

As iron sharpens iron,
so a friend sharpens a friend.
PROVERBS 27:17 NLT

What challenges are there in maintaining great friendships?

A friend loves at all times.
PROVERBS 17:17 NIV

Section 11:

Role models are part of my story.

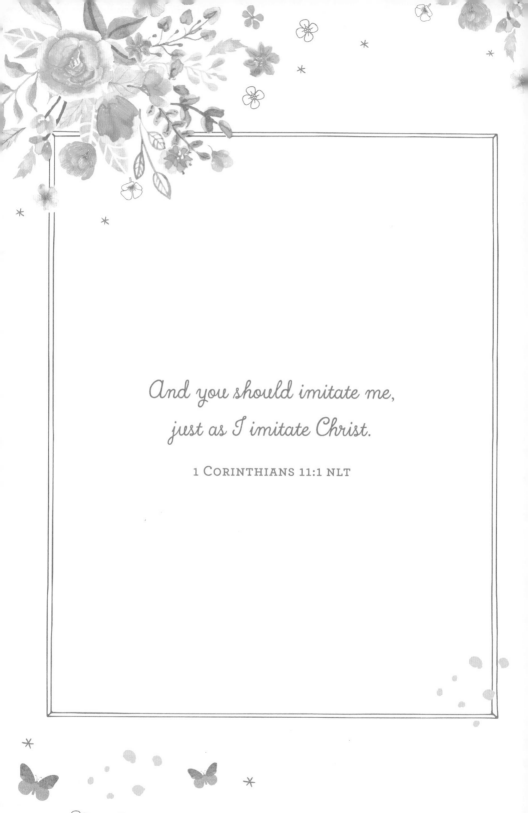

And you should imitate me,
just as I imitate Christ.

1 CORINTHIANS 11:1 NLT

List the names of leaders, mentors, and coaches in your life who made a huge impact on you. How have they helped change your life for the better?

List any modern-day celebrities whom you admire and why.

I am most inspired by these Christian heroes of the faith: ....

....

....

....

....

....

....

....

....

....

....

....

....

....

....

....

....

....

....

....

....

*By faith these people overthrew kingdoms, ruled with
justice, and received what God had promised them.*
HEBREWS 11:33 NLT

Describe a couple who inspires you because of their great marriage. What makes you want to imitate them?

Share about the people you are most looking
forward to meeting or seeing again in heaven.

How do you keep this proper perspective: all human role models will likely fail. . .and only Jesus Christ is your perfect example?

....

....

....

....

....

....

....

....

....

....

....

....

....

....

....

....

....

....

Imitate God, therefore, in everything you do, because you are his dear children. Live a life filled with love, following the example of Christ. He loved us and offered himself as a sacrifice for us, a pleasing aroma to God.

EPHESIANS 5:1–2 NLT

Section 12:

The places I've lived are part of my story.

"The God who made the world and everything in it is the Lord of heaven and earth and does not live in temples built by human hands. . . . From one man he made all the nations, that they should inhabit the whole earth; and he marked out their appointed times in history and the boundaries of their lands. God did this so that they would seek him and perhaps reach out for him and find him, though he is not far from any one of us. 'For in him we live and move and have our being.'"

ACTS 17:24, 26–28 NIV

.... is the place I was born.

List all the places you have lived since you were born.

....

....

....

....

....

....

Have you moved around a lot? Why or why not?

....

....

....

....

....

....

....

....

....

....

....

....

....

The place I've lived that I loved the most is ....
Why? ....

....

....

....

....

....

....

....

....

....

....

....

....

....

....

....

....

....

....

....

....

....

....

The place I've lived that I disliked the most is ....
Why? ....

....

....

....

....

....

....

....

....

....

....

....

....

....

....

....

....

....

....

....

How have the different places you've lived
helped to develop you into the person you are?

....
....
....
....
....
....
....
....
....

How will the places you live continue to develop you in the future?

....
....
....
....
....
....
....
....
....
....
....
....

If I could live anywhere, it would be ....

Why? ....

....

....

....

....

....

....

....

....

....

....

....

....

....

....

....

....

....

....

....

....

....

....

My dream home would be ....
....
....
....
....
....
....
....
....

It would have these features: ....
....
....
....
....
....
....
....
....
....
....
....
....
....
....

Section 13:

My interests and hobbies are part of my story.

Delight yourself in the LORD,
and he will give you
the desires of your heart.

PSALM 37:4 ESV

List the pets you have now or have had in the past.

Describe your favorite things about each pet.

I play/have played these sports:

....

....

....

....

....

....

I play/have played these musical instruments:

....

....

....

....

....

My hobbies are

....

....

....

....

How did you first become interested in these activities?

....

....

....

....

....

Do you love to travel? Why or why not?

....
....
....
....
....
....
....

Do you frequently travel to the same places? . . .

....
....
....
....
....

Or do you like to experience a different place each time you travel?

....
....
....
....
....
....
....
....

List all the places you have traveled to—for work and/or pleasure.

....
....
....
....
....
....
....
....
....

Do you prefer road trips or flights and why?

....
....
....
....
....
....
....

*Look here, you who say, "Today or tomorrow we are going to
a certain town and will stay there a year. We will do business
there and make a profit." How do you know what your life
will be like tomorrow? Your life is like the morning fog—it's
here a little while, then it's gone. What you ought to say is,
"If the Lord wants us to, we will live and do this or that."*
JAMES 4:13–15 NLT

If your budget had no limit, where would
you travel for vacation and why?

List your favorite books.
Describe why they are so meaningful to you.

List your favorite kinds of music and musicians.
Describe what you like best about each.

....
....
....
....
....
....
....
....
....
....
....
....
....
....
....
....
....
....
....

Oh come, let us sing to the LORD*; let us make
a joyful noise to the rock of our salvation!*
PSALM 95:1 ESV

List your favorite TV shows and movies.
What do you enjoy most about them?

I .... (do or do not) like to cook

because ....

....

....

....

....

My favorite foods are ....

....

....

....

....

My least favorite foods are ....

....

....

....

....

My favorite restaurants are ....

....

....

....

....

....

.... always makes me smile.

.... always makes me laugh.

.... always makes me cry.

.... always makes me angry.

.... always frustrates me.

.... always bores me.

.... always excites me.

.... always exhausts me.

.... always energizes me.

....

....

....

....

....

....

....

....

....

....

....

....

....

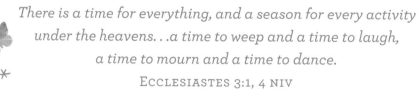

There is a time for everything, and a season for every activity
under the heavens. . .a time to weep and a time to laugh,
a time to mourn and a time to dance.
ECCLESIASTES 3:1, 4 NIV

My favorite board games to play are ....

My favorite crafty thing to do is ....

My favorite social media site is ....

My favorite news source is ....

My favorite magazine is ....

My favorite emoji is ....

My favorite thing to do on a rainy day is ....

My favorite thing to do on a sunny day is ....

My favorite way to exercise is ....

Are you doing a good job taking care of your health, or do you

need to make major improvements? How could you improve?

....

....

....

....

....

....

....

....

....

....

....

....

....

....

....

....

....

....

*For physical training is of some value, but godliness
has value for all things, holding promise for
both the present life and the life to come.*
1 TIMOTHY 4:8 NIV

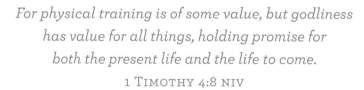

List your favorite holidays.

What are some of your favorite holiday traditions?

Do you make a big deal about birthdays—either yours or others'?
How do you like to celebrate?

....
....
....
....
....
....
....
....
....
....

Share a memory of a favorite birthday celebration.

....
....
....
....
....
....
....
....
....

My favorite season of the year is ....

because ....

....

....

....

....

....

....

....

....

....

....

....

....

....

....

....

....

....

....

....

....

*For everything there is a season, and a
time for every matter under heaven.*
ECCLESIASTES 3:1 ESV

179

Describe the best gift you've ever received.
Who gave it to you? Was it for a special occasion?

....
....
....
....
....
....
....
....
....
....
....
....
....
....
....
....
....
....

*Every good gift and every perfect gift is from above,
coming down from the Father of lights, with whom
there is no variation or shadow due to change.*

JAMES 1:17 ESV

Section 14:

My struggles and triumphs are part of my story.

Three different times I begged the Lord to take it away. Each time he said, "My grace is all you need. My power works best in weakness." So now I am glad to boast about my weaknesses, so that the power of Christ can work through me. That's why I take pleasure in my weaknesses, and in the insults, hardships, persecutions, and troubles that I suffer for Christ. For when I am weak, then I am strong.

2 CORINTHIANS 12:8–10 NLT

This is what stresses me out the most in life:

....

....

....

....

....

....

....

....

....

Describe how you take care of yourself
after an extremely stressful day.

....

....

....

....

....

....

....

....

....

....

Cast all your anxiety on him because he cares for you.
1 PETER 5:7 NIV

I've had these major illnesses and injuries in my life:

....

....

....

....

....

....

I have had these surgeries in my life:

....

....

....

....

....

....

How did God carry you through your health problems?
What did you learn from these experiences?

....

....

....

....

....

....

The worst trials and hardships I have experienced are ....
....
....
....
....
....
....
....
....

How did God strengthen and help you through these
hard things? What did He teach you that you
would never have learned otherwise?

....
....
....
....
....
....
....
....
....
....
....
....

Share your "most embarrassing moment" story.

....

....

....

....

....

....

....

....

....

....

....

....

....

....

....

....

....

Dear brothers and sisters, when troubles of any kind come your way, consider it an opportunity for great joy. For you know that when your faith is tested, your endurance has a chance to grow. So let it grow, for when your endurance is fully developed, you will be perfect and complete, needing nothing.

JAMES 1:2–4 NLT

Describe the worst mistake you've ever made.

....
....
....
....
....
....

How did it get resolved? How did God help you through it?
What did you learn from it?

....
....
....
....
....
....
....
....
....
....
....
....

*If we confess our sins, he is faithful and just to forgive us
our sins and to cleanse us from all unrighteousness.*
1 JOHN 1:9 ESV

What are your deepest fears?

....
....
....
....
....
....

What causes you the most anxiety?

....
....
....
....
....
....

In what ways do you strive to give all your worries
over to God and let His peace rule over you?

....
....
....
....
....
....

Section 15:

God will continue to work in my life. . .for *all* my days.

Being confident of this,
that he who began a good
work in you will carry it
on to completion until the
day of Christ Jesus.

PHILIPPIANS 1:6 NIV

God is still helping to write the story of me.
Here is how I want my story to continue...

JOURNAL ALONGSIDE YOUR DAUGHTER!

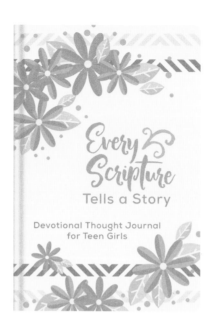

*Every Scripture Tells a Story Devotional
Thought Journal for Teen Girls*

Whether you think about it often or not, God's Word is woven into
your very own amazing story—the story of YOU! The unique
Every Scripture Tells a Story Devotional Thought Journal features
prompts tied into specific scripture selections that will help you
begin to write out your personal story and to see how the very
Word of God speaks truth and love into your life today (and,
in fact, from the very moment God first thought of you!).

Hardback / 978-1-68322-860-8 / $14.99